LOVE SONGS

MELODY LINE, CHORDS AND LYRICS
FOR KEYBOARD • GUITAR • VOCAL

HAL•LEONARD•

ISBN 0-634-01227-4

7777 W. BLUEMOUND RD. P.O. BOX 13819 MILWAUKEE, WI 53213

Visit Hal Leonard Online at
www.halleonard.com

Welcome to the PAPERBACK SONGS SERIES.

Do you play piano, guitar, electronic keyboard, sing or play any instrument for that matter? If so, this handy "pocket tune" book is for you.

The concise, one-line music notation consists of:

MELODY, LYRICS & CHORD SYMBOLS

Whether strumming the chords on guitar, "faking" an arrangement on piano/keyboard or singing the lyrics, these fake book style arrangements can be enjoyed at any experience level — hobbyist to professional.

The musical skills necessary to successfully use this book are minimal. If you play guitar and need some help with chords, a basic chord chart is included at the back of the book.

While playing and singing is the first thing that comes to mind when using this book, it can also serve as a compact, comprehensive reference guide.

However you choose to use this PAPERBACK SONGS SERIES book, by all means have fun!

CONTENTS

(contents continued)

BEAUTIFUL IN MY EYES

Words and Music by
JOSHUA KADISON

Moderately (not too fast)

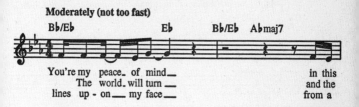

You're my peace of mind___ in this
The world will turn___ and the
lines up-on___ my face___ from a

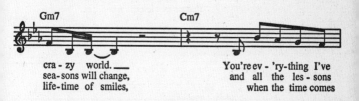

cra-zy world.___ You're ev-'ry-thing I've
sea-sons will change, and all the les-sons
life-time of smiles, when the time comes

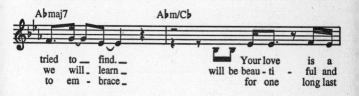

tried to ___ find. ___ Your love is a
we will ___ learn ___ will be beau-ti-___ ful and
to em - brace ___ for one long last

pearl. _____ You're my
strange. _____ We'll have our
while; _____ we can

8

Mo - na Li - sa, you're my_ rain - bow skies,_ and my_
fill of tears,_ our_ share_ of sighs._ My_
laugh a - bout_ how time real - ly flies._ We won't_

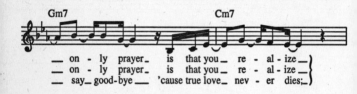

_ on - ly prayer_ is that you_ re - al - ize_
_ on - ly prayer_ is that you_ re - al - ize
_ say_ good - bye_ 'cause true love_ nev - er dies;_

you'll al - ways be_ Beau - ti - ful_ In My

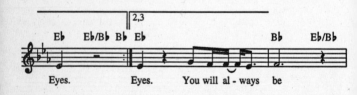

Eyes. Eyes. You will al - ways be

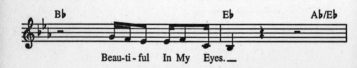

Beau - ti - ful In My Eyes._

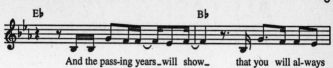

And the pass-ing years _ will show _ that you will al-ways

grow _ ev - er more _ Beau-ti - ful _____

In My Eyes. When there are

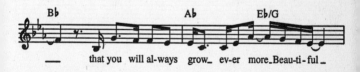

Eyes. The pass - ing years _ will show _

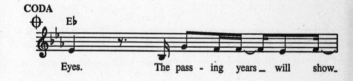

_ that you will al-ways grow _ ev-er more _ Beau-ti - ful _

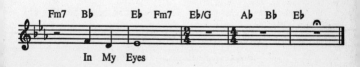

In My Eyes

ALL I ASK OF YOU
from THE PHANTOM OF THE OPERA

Music by ANDREW LLOYD WEBBER
Lyrics by CHARLES HART
Additional Lyrics by RICHARD STILGOE

Moderately slow

RAOUL

No more talk of dark-ness, for - get these wide-eyed fears: I'm

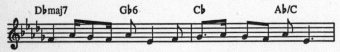

here, noth-ing can harm you, my words will warm and calm you.

Let me be your free - dom; let

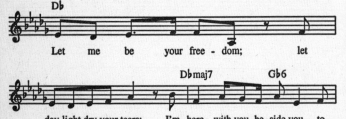

day-light dry your tears: I'm here, with you, be-side you, to

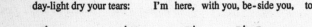

CHRISTINE

guard you and to guide you. Say you love me ev - 'ry

wak - ing mo-ment; turn my head with talk of

E♭m7 E♭m7/A♭ D♭ B♭m7

sum-mer-time. Say you need me with you

E♭m7 A♭ D♭/F G♭

now and al-ways; pro-mise me that all you say is

D♭/A♭ E♭m/A♭ A♭6 E♭m/A♭

true; that's All I Ask Of

D♭
RAOUL

You.
Let me be your shel-ter; let me be your light. You're

D♭maj7 G♭6 C♭ A♭/C

safe; no one will find you; your fears are far be-hind you.

D♭
CHRISTINE

All I want is free - dom, a

D♭maj7 G♭6

world with no more night; and you, al-ways be-side me, to

12

Cb   **Ab/C**   *RAOUL* **Db**   **Bbm7**

hold me and to hide me. Then say you'll share with me one

Ebm7   **Ab**   **Db/F**   **Bbm7**

love, one life-time; let me lead you from your

Ebm7   **Ab Ab6 Ab7 Db**   **Bbm7**

so - li - tude. _ Say you need me with you,

Ebm7   **Ab**   **Db/F**   **Gb**

here be - side you. An-y-where you go, let me go

Db/Ab   **Ebm7/Ab**   **Ab6**   **Ebm7/Ab**

too. Chris - tine, that's All I Ask Of

Db   **Bbm7**   **Ebm7**   **Ab**
CHRISTINE

You.
Say you'll share with me one love, one life-time;

Db/F   **Bbm7**   **Ebm7**   **Ebm7/Ab**

say the word and I will fol-low you. _

ALWAYS

Words and Music by
IRVING BERLIN

Moderate Waltz

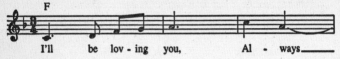

I'll be lov-ing you, Al - ways____

____ with a love that's true,

Al - ways. ____ When the things you've

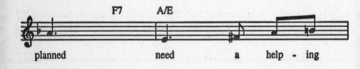

planned need a help - ing

hand, I will un - der -

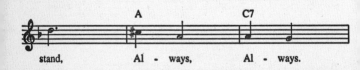

stand, Al - ways, Al - ways.

Days may not be fair, Al - ways. ___

___ That's when I'll be there,

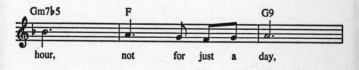

Al - ways, ___ not for just an

hour, not for just a day,

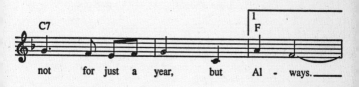

not for just a year, but Al - ways. ___

___ Al - ways. ___

ALWAYS ON MY MIND

Words and Music by WAYNE THOMPSON, MARK JAMES and JOHNNY CHRISTOPHER

17

AND I LOVE HER

Words and Music by
JOHN LENNON and PAUL McCARTNEY

I give her all my love,
She gives me ev-'ry-thing
Bright are the stars that shine,

that's all I do.
and ten-der-ly.
dark is the sky.

And if you saw my love
The kiss my lov-er brings
I know this love of mine

you'd love her too.
she brings to me.
will nev-er die.

I love her.
And I Love Her.
And I Love Her.

A love like ours

could nev-er die as long as I

G#m   B   D.C. al Coda

have you   near me.

CODA

Gm

Instrumental ad lib.
Bright   are   the   stars

Dm   Gm   Dm

that shine, _   dark is the sky.

Gm   Dm   Bb

I know this love of mine _____ will nev-er die, _

C   1.
             F6

And I Love _ Her. _

2.
F6   Gm

Her. _   *(Instrumental)*

F6

Gm   D

AND SO IT GOES

Words and Music by
BILLY JOEL

Slow Ballad

In ev - 'ry heart _____ there is a
you _____ in cau - tious

room, a sanc - tu - ar - y safe and
tones; you an - swered me with no pre -

strong. _____ To heal the
tense. _____ And still I

wounds _____ from lov - ers past, un -
feel _____ I said too much. My

til a new one comes a - long. _____ I spoke to
si - lence is my self de - fense. _____ And ev - 'ry

time _____ I've held a rose _____ it seems I _____

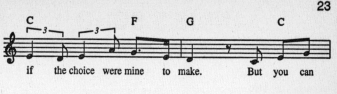

if the choice were mine to make. But you can

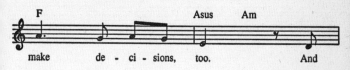

make de - ci - sions, too. And

you can have this heart to break. __ (Instrumental)

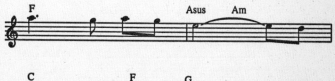

And So It Goes, __

__ And So It Goes, __ and you're the

on - ly __ one who knows. ____

ANNIE'S SONG

Words and Music by
JOHN DENVER

You fill up my sens -

es _____ like a night in a

for - est, _____ Like the

moun - tains in spring - time, _____

_____ like a walk in the

rain. _____ Like a

storm in the des - ert, _____

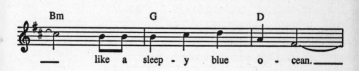

like a sleep - y blue o - cean. ___

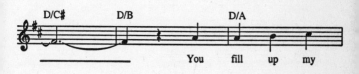

You fill up my

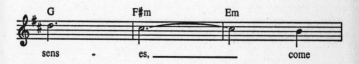

sens - es, _____ come

fill me a - gain. _____

26

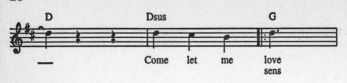

D   **Dsus**   **G**

—   Come   let   me   love
                       sens

A   **Bm**   **G**

you, _____   let   me   give   my   life
es _____   like   a   night   in   a

D   **D/C#**   **D/B**

to   you. _____   Let   me
for - est. _____   Like   the

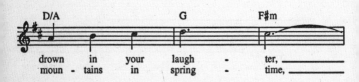

D/A   **G**   **F#m**

drown   in   your   laugh - ter, _____
moun - tains   in   spring - time, _____

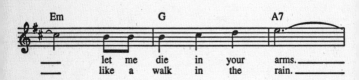

Em   **G**   **A7**

—   let   me   die   in   your   arms. _____
—   like   a   walk   in   the   rain. _____

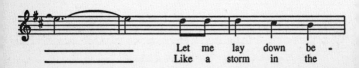

_____   Let   me   lay   down   be -
_____   Like   a   storm   down   in   the

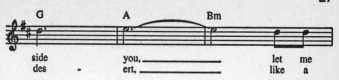

side   you,____   let me
des - ert,____   like a

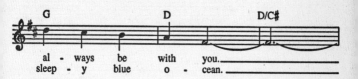

al - ways be with you.____
sleep - y blue o - cean.____

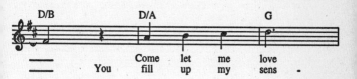

____   Come let me love
____   You fill up my sens -

you,____   come love me a -
es,____   come fill me a -

gain.____   You fill up my

gain.____

BEAUTY AND THE BEAST

from Walt Disney's BEAUTY AND THE BEAST

Lyrics by HOWARD ASHMAN
Music by ALAN MENKEN

CAN YOU FEEL
THE LOVE TONIGHT
from Walt Disney Pictures' THE LION KING

Music by ELTON JOHN
Lyrics by TIM RICE

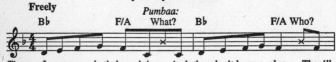

Timon: I can see what's hap-p'ning. And they don't have a clue. They'll

fall in love and here's the bot-tom line: Our tri-o's down to two. The

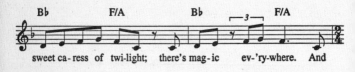

sweet ca-ress of twi-light; there's mag-ic ev-'ry-where. And

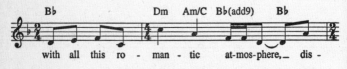

with all this ro- man- tic at-mos-phere,__ dis-

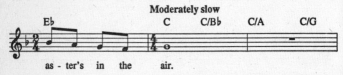

as- ter's in the air.

Chorus:
Can You Feel__ The Love__ To - night,__

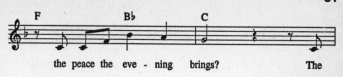

the peace the eve - ning brings? The

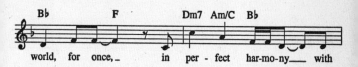

world, for once, _ in per - fect har-mo-ny___ with

all its liv - ing things. _ *Simba:* So

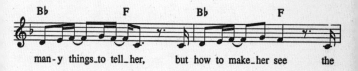

man - y things _ to tell _ her, but how to make _ her see the

truth a-bout _ my past? _ Im-pos-si-ble. She'd turn a-way from me. *Nala:* He's

hold-ing back, _ he's hid - ing. But what? I can't _ de-cide. _ Why

32

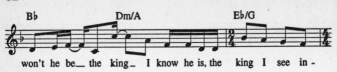

won't he be the king I know he is, the king I see in-

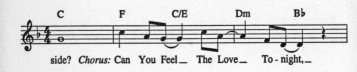

side? *Chorus:* Can You Feel The Love To - night,

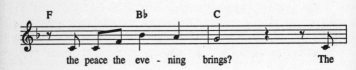

the peace the eve - ning brings? The

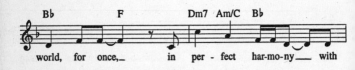

world, for once, in per - fect har-mo-ny with

all its liv - ing things. Can You Feel The Love

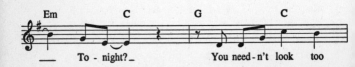

To - night? You need-n't look too

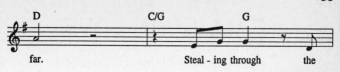

far.   Steal - ing through   the

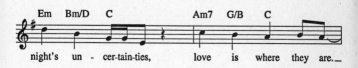

night's   un - cer-tain-ties,   love   is   where   they   are._

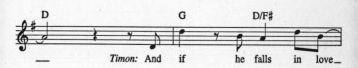

_   *Timon:* And   if   he   falls   in   love_

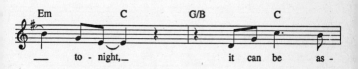

_   to - night,_   it   can   be   as -

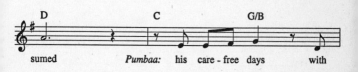

sumed   *Pumbaa:* his   care - free   days   with

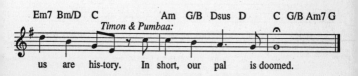

us   are   his-tory.   In   short,   our   pal   is   doomed.

CAN'T HELP FALLING IN LOVE

**Words and Music by GEORGE DAVID WEISS,
HUGO PERETTI and LUIGI CREATORE**

Moderately slow

F · Am · Dm
Wise · men · say · on-ly

Bb · F · C7
fools · rush · in, ___ · but

Bb · C · Dm · Gm
I · Can't · Help · Fall-ing · In

F/C · C7 · F · Am
Love · with · you. · Shall · I

Dm · Bb · F
stay? · Would · it · be · a

C7 · Bb · C
sin ___ · if · I · Can't

Dm · Gm · F/C · C7 · F
Help · Fall-ing · In · Love · with · you?

CHANGE THE WORLD

featured on the Motion Picture Soundtrack PHENOMENON

Words and Music by GORDON KENNEDY,
WAYNE KIRKPATRICK and TOMMY SIMS

38

THE COLOUR OF MY LOVE

**Words and Music by DAVID FOSTER
and ARTHUR JANOV**

G♭maj7　A♭9sus A♭7　Db

hold each oth-er,　oh, so　tight.

G♭maj7

I'll paint a　sun to warm your heart, swear-ing that we'll.

Fm7　B♭m7　E♭m7　A♭7sus　A♭7

__ nev-er part. ___　That's The Col-our Of___ My

Db(add9)　Db/F　G♭maj7

Love.　I'll paint the truth_　show how I feel,　try to make you_

Fm7　B♭m7

__ com-plete-ly real. _____　I'll use a

E♭m7　Fm7　G♭maj7　A♭9sus A♭7

brush so light and fine　to draw you close　and make you

Db　G♭/Db A♭/Db Db　Cm7

mine.　I'll paint a

Fmaj7

sun　to　warm your heart,　swear-ing that we'll_

CHERISH

Words and Music by
TERRY KIRKMAN

Moderately

Cher-ish is the word I use to de-scribe
Per-ish is the word that more than ap-plies

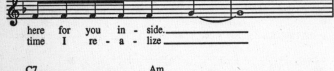

all the feel-ing that I have hid-ing
to the hope in my heart each

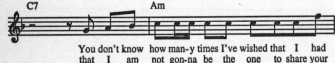

here for you in-side.
time I re-a-lize

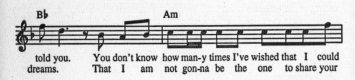

You don't know how man-y times I've wished that I had
that I am not gon-na be the one to share your

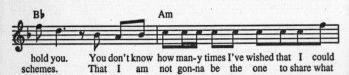

told you. You don't know how man-y times I've wished that I could
dreams. That I am not gon-na be the one to share your

hold you. You don't know how man-y times I've wished that I could
schemes. That I am not gon-na be the one to share what

To Coda ⊕

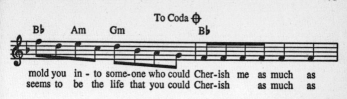

mold you in - to some-one who could Cher-ish me as much as
seems to be the life that you could Cher-ish as much as

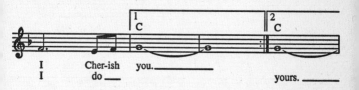

I Cher-ish you._____
I do __

yours. _____

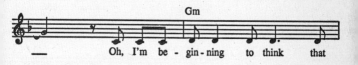

__ Oh, I'm be - gin-ning to think that

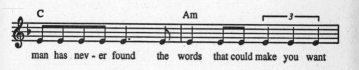

man has nev - er found the words that could make you want

me. That have the right a - mount of let - ters,

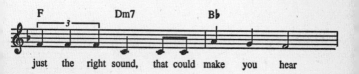

just the right sound, that could make you hear

44

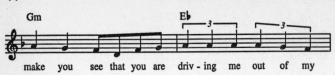

Gm   Eb

make you see that you are driv-ing me out of my

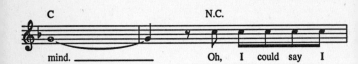

C   N.C.

mind. _____ Oh, I could say I

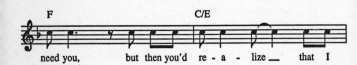

F   C/E

need you, but then you'd re - a - lize __ that I

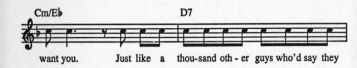

Cm/Eb   D7

want you. Just like a thou-sand oth - er guys who'd say they

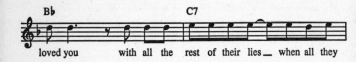

Bb   C7

loved you with all the rest of their lies __ when all they

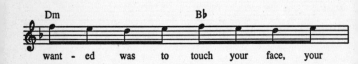

Dm   Bb

want - ed was to touch your face, your

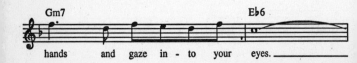

Gm7   Eb6

hands and gaze in - to your eyes. _____

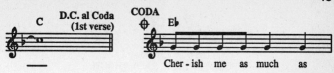

D.C. al Coda
(1st verse)

CODA

Cher - ish me as much as

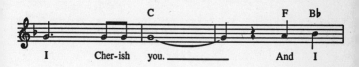

I Cher-ish you. _____ And I

do _____ Cher - ish you. _____

_ And I do _____

_ Cher - ish you. _____

_ Cher-ish is the word. _____

(They Long to Be)
CLOSE TO YOU

Lyric by HAL DAVID
Music by BURT BACHARACH

Why do birds sud-den-ly ap-pear ev-'ry-time you are near. Just like me,__ They Long To Be Close To You.__ Why do stars fall down from the sky ev-'ry time you walk by. Just like me,__ They Long To Be Close To You.__

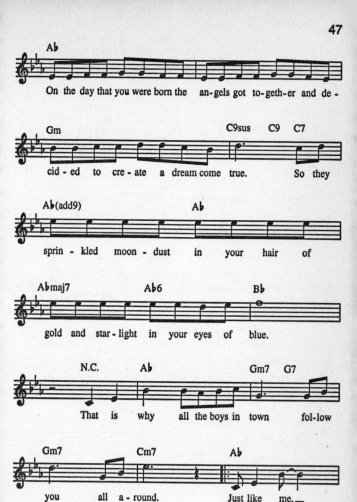

On the day that you were born the an-gels got to-geth-er and de-

cid-ed to cre-ate a dream come true. So they

sprin-kled moon-dust in your hair of

gold and star-light in your eyes of blue.

That is why all the boys in town fol-low

you all a-round. Just like me,

Repeat and Fade

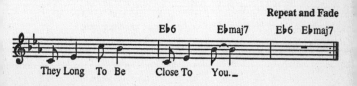

They Long To Be Close To You.

DON'T KNOW MUCH

Words and Music by BARRY MANN, CYNTHIA WEIL and TOM SNOW

Tenderly

Look at this face, I know the years are show-ing.

Look at this life, _____ I

still don't know where it's go-ing. I Don't Know_ Much,

but I know I love you, _____ and

that may be _____ all I need _ to

know. Look at these eyes,

they've nev-er seen what mat-ters.__ Look at these dreams,__

so beat-en__ and so bat-tered. _____ I Don't Know__ Much,

but I know I love you, _____ and

that may be _____ all I need __ to know.

So man-y ques-tions still left un-an-swered.

So much I've nev-er bro-ken through. __

And when I feel you near me some-times I see so clear-ly

the on - ly truth I've ev - er known ___ is me and you. __

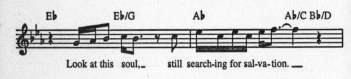

Look at this man, so blessed with in-spi-ra-tion.. __

Look at this soul, __ still search-ing for sal-va-tion. __

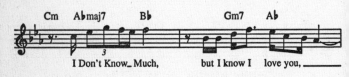

I Don't Know_ Much, but I know I love you, _____

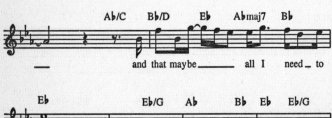

___ and that maybe_____ all I need _ to

know.

EASY

Words and Music by
LIONEL RICHIE

Moderately

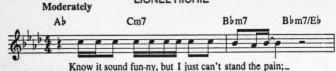

Know it sound fun-ny, but I just can't stand the pain;—

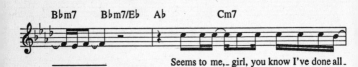

girl, I'm leav - ing you ___ to - mor - row.—

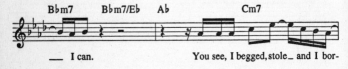

___ Seems to me,— girl, you know I've done all.—

___ I can.   You see, I begged, stole— and I bor-

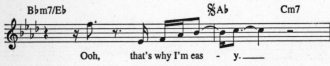

- rowed, ____   yeah. ____

Ooh,   that's why I'm eas - y. ____

Bbm7   Bbm7/Eb

I'm eas - y like Sun - day morn -

- ing.

That's why I'm eas -

- y.

I'm eas - y like Sun - day morn -

To Coda ⊕

- ing.

Why in the world would an-y-bod-y put chains on me?

I've paid my dues to make it.

Ev - 'ry - bod - y wants me to be what they want

- me to be.

I'm not hap - py when I try to fake

(Instrumental)

(Instrumental)

That's why I'm eas - y. ___

I'm eas - y like Sun - day morn -

- ing. That's why I'm eas -

y. ___

___ I'm eas - y like Sun - day morn -

Repeat and Fade

- ing. ___ 'Cause I'm eas -

ENDLESS LOVE

from ENDLESS LOVE

Words and Music by
LIONEL RICHIE

57

CODA

And yes _____

you'll be the on - ly _ one. _____

Oh, no _____ I can't de - ny_

this love _____ I have in - side_

and I'll give _____ it all to

you my love _____

my End - less Love. _____

EV'RY TIME
WE SAY GOODBYE
from SEVEN LIVELY ARTS

Words and Music by
COLE PORTER

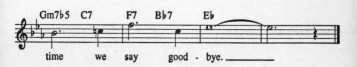

THE FIRST TIME EVER I SAW YOUR FACE

Words and Music by
EWAN MacCOLL

Slowly

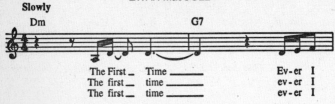

The First _ Time _____ Ev-er I
The first _ time _____ ev-er I
The first _ time _____ ev-er I

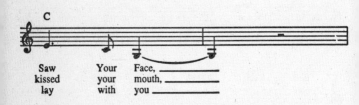

Saw   Your   Face, _____
kissed your   mouth, _____
lay   with   you _____

I thought _ the sun _____ rose
I felt _____ the earth _____ move.
and felt ____ your heart _____ so ___

___   in your eyes. _____
___   in my hand. _____
___   close to mine. _____

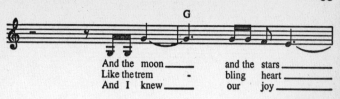

G

And the moon____ and the stars____
Like the trem - bling heart____
And I knew____ our joy____

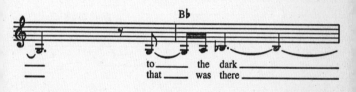

G7   **C**   To Coda ⊕

were the gifts you gave____
of a cap - tive bird____
would fill the earth____

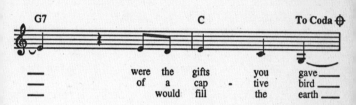

B♭

to____ the dark____
that____ was there____

and the end of the
at my com -

1
C   2
         C   D.C. al Coda

skies.   mand,   my love.

64

CODA

and last   till the end

of time,   my love.   The First Time

Ev-er I Saw

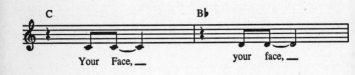

Your Face,   your face,

your face,   your face.

HERE AND NOW

Words and Music by TERRY STEELE and DAVID ELLIOT

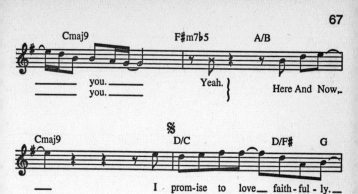

you.
you.
Yeah.
Here And Now,

I prom-ise to love faith-ful-ly.

You're all I need.

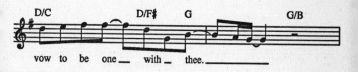

Here And Now, I

vow to be one with thee.

To Coda

Your love is all

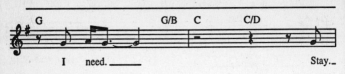

I need. _____ Stay. _

When

Your love is all _____ I need. _____ Start-ing here. _

_ Ooh, and I'm _ start - ing _ now. _____ I be - lieve. _

Start - ing here. _____
I be - lieve. _

_ I'm start - ing right here. Start - ing now. _____

A GROOVY KIND OF LOVE

Words and Music by TONI WINE
and CAROLE BAYER SAGER

When I'm feel-in' blue, all I have to
want to you can turn me

do is take a look at you, then I'm not so
on to an-y-thing you want to, an-y-time at

blue. When you're close to me I can feel your
all. When I taste your lips oh, I start to

heart beat I can hear you breath-ing in my
shiv-er can't con-trol the quiv-er-ing in-

ear.}
side.} Would-n't you a-gree, ba-by, you and

me got A Groov-y Kind Of Love.

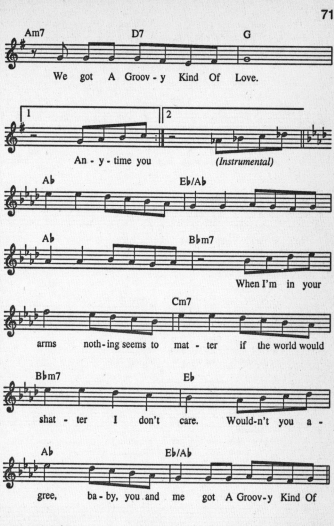

We got A Groov-y Kind Of Love.

[1.] An - y - time you

[2.] (Instrumental)

When I'm in your arms noth-ing seems to mat - ter if the world would shat - ter I don't care. Would-n't you a - gree, ba - by, you and me got A Groov-y Kind Of Love.

We got A Groov-y Kind Of

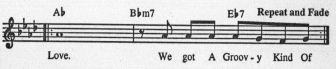

Repeat and Fade

GROW OLD WITH ME

Words and Music by
JOHN LENNON

Moderate Ballad

Grow old a - long with me ___ The
old a - long with me ___ Two
old a - long with me ___ What-

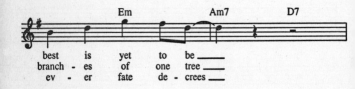

best is yet to be ___
branch - es of one tree ___
ev - er fate de - crees ___

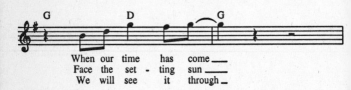

When our time has come ___
Face the set - ting sun ___
We will see it through ___

We will be as one ___
When the day is done ___
For our love is true ___

God bless our love ___

HERE, THERE AND EVERYWHERE

Words and Music by
JOHN LENNON and PAUL McCARTNEY

Am7 D F7 Bb Gm

— I want her ev - 'ry-where and if

Cm D7 Gm

she's be - side me I know I need nev - er care.

Cm D7 G Am7

But to love her is to need her ev - 'ry - where, _

Bm C G Am7

know - ing that love _ is to share; _

Bm C F#m7 B7

each one be - liev - ing that love _ nev - er dies, _

F#m7 B7 Em Am 1. Am7 D F7

watch-ing her eyes _ and hop - ing I'm al - ways there. _ I want her

2. Am7 D7sus G Am Bm C

_ I will be there and ev - 'ry - where, _

G Am7 Bm C G

Here, There And Ev - 'ry - where. _

HOW DEEP IS THE OCEAN
(How High Is the Sky)

Words and Music by
IRVING BERLIN

Slowly

How much do I love you?

I'll tell you no lie.

How Deep Is The O - cean,

how high is the sky?

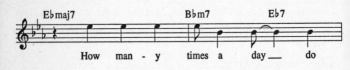

How man - y times a day __ do

I think of you? __ How man - y ros -

I BELIEVE IN YOU AND ME

from the Touchstone Motion Picture THE PREACHER'S WIFE

Words and Music by DAVID WOLFERT
and SANDY LINZER

like the riv - er finds ___ the sea, I ___ was

lost, ___ now I'm _ free ___ 'cause

I Be - lieve _ In You _ And Me. I will nev - er leave _

___ your side. _ I will nev - er hurt _ your _ pride. _ When all the

chips are down, ___ babe, then I will

al - ways be _ a - round. _ Just to be right where you are, _

___ my love. ___ You know I love _

Dm7   F/G   C
you, boy. I'll nev-er leave_you out._ I will al-ways

C/Bb
let you in, boy, oh, ba - by, to

Fmaj7/A
pla - ces no one's ev - er been.

Ab/Bb   Bb7
_ Deep _____ in - side, _____

C/G   Em7   Am7
_____ can't you see _____ that

Dm7   F/G   C
I Be - lieve _ In You _____ And Me.

Em7   Am7
May - be I'm a fool _____ to

I FINALLY FOUND SOMEONE

from THE MIRROR HAS TWO FACES

Words and Music by BARBRA STREISAND,
MARVIN HAMLISCH, R.J. LANGE
and BRYAN ADAMS

Moderately slow

Male: I Fi-n'lly Found Some-one who knocks me off my feet. I fi-n'lly found the one_ that makes me feel com-plete.

Female: It start-ed o-ver cof-fee. We start-ed out as friends. It's fun-ny how from sim-ple things_ the best things be-gin._

Male: This time it's dif-f'rent. It's all be-cause of you._ It's bet-ter than it's ev-er been_

84

'cause we can talk it through. *Female:* My fav-'rite line_ was, "Can I call you some - time?"_ It's all you had to say _ to take my breath a - way._ *Both:* This is it. Oh,_ I Fi - n'lly Found Some-one, some-one to share_ my life. I fi-n'lly found the one_ to be with ev-'ry night. *Female:* 'Cause what-ev - er I do,_ *Male:* it's just

C#m   C   E/B

got to be you. *Both:* My life has just be-gun. I Fi-n'lly

F#m7/B   E

Found   Some - one. ___

C#m7   Amaj7

(Instrumental)

E/F#   F#   B

Male: Did I keep you wait - ing?
        Female: I did - n't mind. __

G#m7

I a - pol - o - gize. Ba - by, that's fine. __

Emaj7

I would wait for - ev - er just to know. __
                      just to know. __

Em6

___ you were mine. ___   You know,
___ you were mine. _____

I LEFT MY HEART
IN SAN FRANCISCO

Words by DOUGLASS CROSS
Music by GEORGE CORY

I Left My Heart In San Fran -

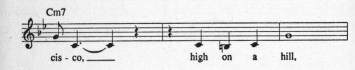

cis - co, _____ high on a hill,

it calls to me. To be where

lit - tle ca-ble cars _____ climb half-way to the stars! _____

_____ The morn - ing fog _____ may chill the

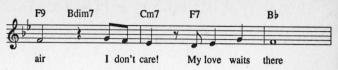

air   I don't care! My love waits there

in San Fran - cis - co, _____ a - bove the

blue _____ and wind - y sea.

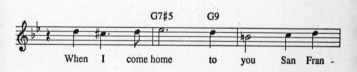

When I come home to you San Fran -

cis - co   your gold - en sun will

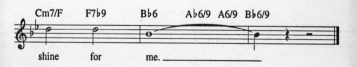

shine for me. _____

I SAY A LITTLE PRAYER

Lyric by HAL DAVID
Music by BURT BACHARACH

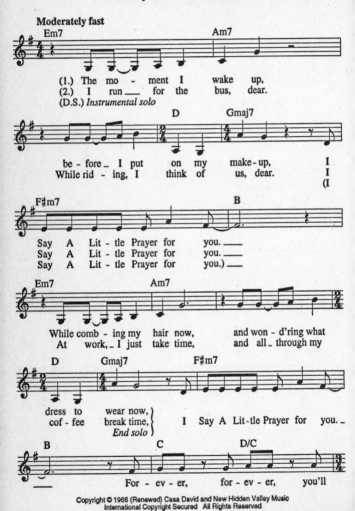

(1.) The mo - ment I wake up,
(2.) I run ___ for the bus, dear.
(D.S.) *Instrumental solo*

be - fore ___ I put on my make - up, I
While rid - ing, I think of us, dear. I
(I

Say A Lit - tle Prayer for you. ___
Say A Lit - tle Prayer for you. ___
Say A Lit - tle Prayer for you.) ___

While comb - ing my hair now, and won - d'ring what
At work, I just take time, and all ___ through my

dress to wear now,)
cof - fee break time,}
End solo}
I Say A Lit - tle Prayer for you. ___

For - ev - er, for - ev - er, you'll

C/D

for me _ there is no one _____ but ____

Gmaj7   Am7/D   Gmaj7

you.   Please _ love me, _ too. _____

Am7/D   Gmaj7   Am7/D

I'm _ in love with   you, _____   an - swer my_

Gmaj7   Am7/D

_ prayer. _____   Say _ you love me,

Gmaj7   Am7/D

too. _____

                    Gmaj7

Why don't you an - swer my   prayer? _____

Am7/D   **Repeat and Fade**

You know, ev - 'ry day I say a lit - tle

I WANT TO SPEND MY LIFETIME LOVING YOU

from the TriStar Motion Picture THE MASK OF ZORRO

Music by JAMES HORNER
Lyric by WILL JENNINGS

Moderately slow

Male: Moon so bright, night so fine, keep your heart here with mine. Life's a dream ____ we are dream - ing. ____ *Female:* Race the moon, _ catch the wind, _ ride the night to the end. _ Seize the day, stand up ____ for the light. *Both:* I Want To Spend My Life - time

Bb — Ebm
Lov-ing You if that is all in

Bb
life I ev - er __ do. __

Ebm/Bb
He - roes __ rise, __ he-roes fall. __ Rise a-gain,

Abm7
win it all. _____ *Female:* In your heart, __

Bb
can't you feel the glo - ry? _____

Through our joy, through our pain, __

Ebm/Gb — Ebm
Both: we can move worlds a - gain. __

Abm
Take my hand, _____ dance __ with

me. *Male:* Dance with me. *Both:* I Want To

Spend My Life - time
noth - ing else to

Lov-ing You if that is all in
see me through if I can

life I ev - er do.

I will want spend my

life - time lov - ing you.

(Instrumental)

Male: Though we know _____ we will nev - er come a - gain, _____ where there is love, _____ **Both:** life be - gins o - ver and o - ver a - gain. _____ Save the night, save the day. Save the love come what may. _____ Love is worth ev - 'ry - thing we pay.

I Want To (1.,2.) Spend My Life - time
(3.) noth - ing else to

Lov - ing You if that is
see me through if I can

1,2

all in life I

ev - er ___ do. ___ { I Want To
{ I will want

3

spend my life - time ___

___ lov - ing ___ you. ___

Slower

(Instrumental)

I WILL

Words and Music by
JOHN LENNON and PAUL McCARTNEY

Who knows _ how long _ I've loved _ you? _ You know _
_ I ev - er saw _ you, _ I did -

_ I love you still. _ Will I wait
- n't catch _ your name, _ But it nev -

_ a lone - ly life - time? If you want
- er real - ly mat - tered, I will al -

_ me to, _ I Will. For if _
- ways feel _ the same. _

Love you for - ev - er and _ for - ev - er,

Love you with all _ my heart, _

Love you when - ev - er we're _ to - geth - er,

I WILL BE HERE

Words and Music by
STEVEN CURTIS CHAPMAN

Gently, but not too slowly

To-mor-row morn-in' if you __ wake up and the
To-mor-row morn-in' if you __ wake up and the

sun does __ not __ ap-pear, __
fu-ture is __ un-clear, __

I, _____ I Will Be Here..
I, _____ I Will Be Here..

If in the dark we __ lose sight __
As sure as sea-sons are made __

__ of __ love, __ hold my __
__ for __ change, __ our

-in', through the win-nin', los - in' and try-
-ty and tell you all the things you are to

-in', we'll be to-geth - er, ___
___ me. I Will Be Here. ___

To Coda ⊕

'cause I Will Be Here. ___

(Instrumental)

CODA
⊕

Hmm ___

D.C. al Coda

I will ___ be ___ true to the prom-

-ise I ___ have ___ made to

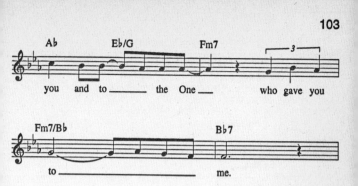

you and to _____ the One _____ who gave you

to _____ me.

(Instrumental)

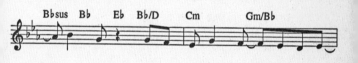

I, _____

— I Will Be Here. _____

And _____ just as sure as sea-sons are made_

104

I WILL REMEMBER YOU
Theme from THE BROTHERS McMULLEN

Words and Music by SARAH McLACHLAN,
SEAMUS EGAN and DAVE MERENDA

I Will Re - mem - ber __ You. __

Will you re - mem - ber __ me? __ Don't

let your life __ pass __ you by. __

Weep not for __ the mem - o - ries. __ Re -

mem - ber the good times that we had. __ We
I'm so tired, but I can't sleep. __
so a - fraid to love you, more a - fraid to lose,

let them slip a - way __ from us when
Stand - in' on the edge of some - thing
cling - ing to a past __ that does - n't

107

I'LL BE THERE

Words and Music by BERRY GORDY,
HAL DAVIS, WILLIE HUTCH and BOB WEST

Moderately

You and I must make a pact.

We must bring sal-va-tion back. _____

Where there is love, _____ I'll

__ be there. (I'll be there.) __

I'll reach out my hand to you,
I'll be there to pro-tect you

I'll have faith in all you do. _____
with an un-self-ish love that re-spects you. _____

Just call my name _____ and I'll __

name _____ and I'll __

__ be there. __

1
C7sus

2 **Freely**
Bb **Gm7** *3*

Just call my name __

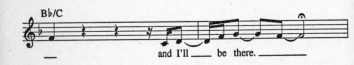

Bb/C

__ and I'll __ be there. __

F **Eb** **Bb**

(Instrumental)

F **Eb** **Bb**

IF

Words and Music by
DAVID GATES

Moderately, with feeling

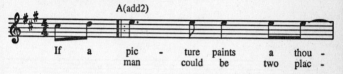

If a pic - ture paints a thou -
man could be two plac -

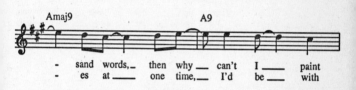

- sand words,_ then why _ can't I _ paint
- es at _ one time,_ I'd be _ with

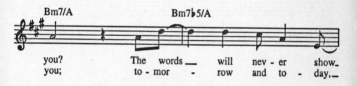

you? The words _ will nev - er show_
you; to - mor - row and to - day,_

_ the you _ I've come_ to know..
_ be - side _ you all _ the way.

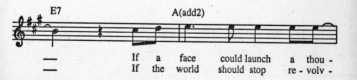

_ If a face could launch a thou -
_ If the world should stop re - volv -

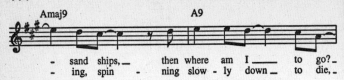

Amaj9   A9

- sand ships,___ then where am I ___ to go?___
- ing, spin - ning slow - ly down ___ to die,___

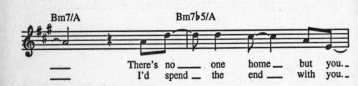

Bm7/A   Bm7♭5/A

There's no ___ one home ___ but you.___
I'd spend ___ the end ___ with you.___

A   Bm7♭5/D

You're all ___ that's left ___ me
And when ___ the world ___ was

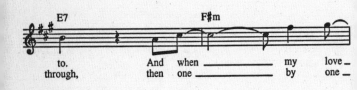

E7   F#m

to.   And when _____ my love
through,   then one _____ by one ___

F#m/E#   F#m/E

_____ for life ___ is run - ning___
_____ the stars ___ would all ___ go ___

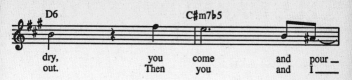

dry,   you   come   and   pour ___
out.   Then   you   and   I ___

___   your   -   self   on
___   would

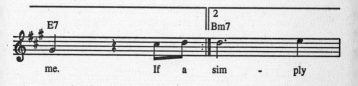

me.   If   a   sim   -   ply

fly   a   -   way. ___

I'LL MAKE LOVE TO YOU

Words and Music by
BABYFACE

Slowly, in a steady 2

Close your eyes, make a wish, and blow
lax, let's go slow. I ain't

out the can - dle - light for to -
got no - where to go. I'm just gonna

night is just your night. We're gon - na
con - cen - trate on you. Girl, are you

cel - e - brate all through the night. Pour the
read-y? It's gonna be a long night. Throw your

wine, light the fire. Girl, your
clothes on the floor I'm gonna

wish is my com - mand. I sub -
take my clothes off too. I made

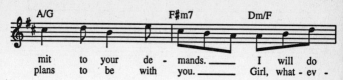

mit to your de - mands. _____ I will do
plans to be with you. _____ Girl, what - ev -

an - y - thing. _____ Girl, you need on - ly ask. } I'll Make
er you ask me, you know I could do. }

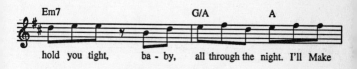

Love To You like you want me to and I'll

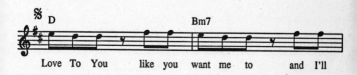

hold you tight, ba - by, all through the night. I'll Make

Love To You when you want me to and I

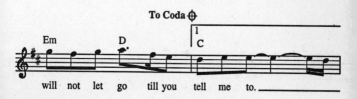

will not let go till you tell me to. _____

Gmaj7/A

_ Girl, re -

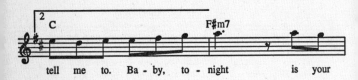

2
C   F#m7

tell me to. Ba - by, to - night   is   your

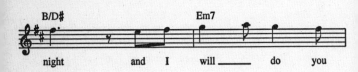

B/D#   Em7

night   and   I   will ____ do   you

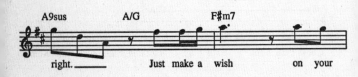

A9sus   A/G   F#m7

right. ____   Just make a   wish   on   your

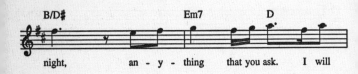

B/D#   Em7   D

night,   an - y - thing that you ask.   I will

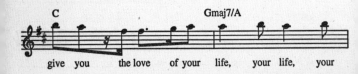

C   Gmaj7/A

give you   the love of your life,   your life,   your

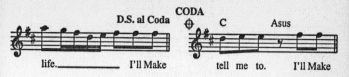

D.S. al Coda   CODA   C   Asus

life._____ I'll Make   tell me to.   I'll Make

D   Bm7

Love To You   like you   want me to   and I'll
(Instrumental ad lib. and Fade)

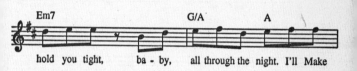

Em7   G/A   A

hold you tight,   ba - by,   all through the night. I'll Make

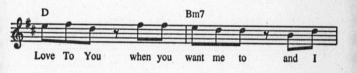

D   Bm7

Love To You   when you   want me to   and I

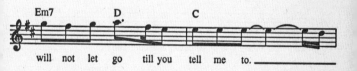

Em7   D   C

will not let go   till you   tell me to. _____

Gmaj7/A   **Repeat ad lib. and Fade**

IF EVER
I WOULD LEAVE YOU

from CAMELOT

Words by ALAN JAY LERNER
Music by FREDERICK LOEWE

Moderately, with expression

121

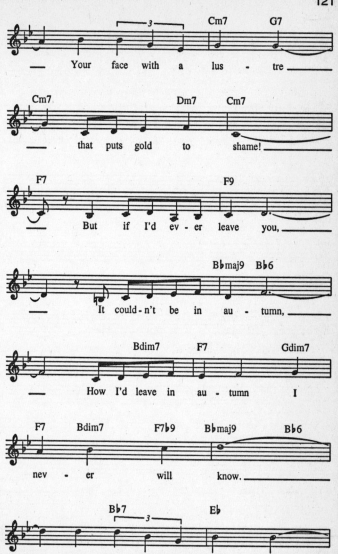

IF I LOVED YOU

from CAROUSEL

Lyrics by OSCAR HAMMERSTEIN II
Music by RICHARD RODGERS

Slowly

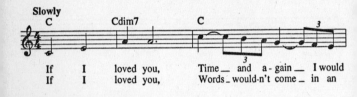

If   I   loved you,   Time _ and a-gain _ I would
If   I   loved you,   Words _ would-n't come _ in an

try   to   say   All   I'd   want you   to
eas - y   way.   'Round   in   cir - cles   I'd

know. _____   go. _____

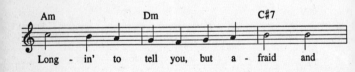

Long - in'   to   tell you, but a - fraid   and

shy, I'd let my gold - en chanc - es

pass me by! Soon you'd

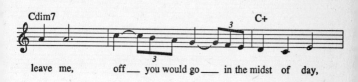

leave me, off___ you would go___ in the midst of day,

Nev - er, nev - er to know___

___ How I loved you,

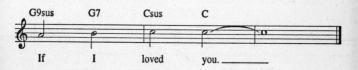

If I loved you.___

IF YOU HAD MY LOVE

Words and Music by RODNEY JERKINS, LaSHAWN DANIELS,
CORY ROONEY, FRED JERKINS and JENNIFER LOPEZ

Moderate steady beat

F#m7

me. _____ Tell me who can I
know. _____ If you wan - na

Bm

trust if I can't trust in you?_ And I re-fuse to
live with all I have to give_ I need to feel true

Em7   F#m7

let you play me for a fool. _____ You said _
love or it's got to end, yeah. __ I don't_

Bm

_ that we _ could pos - si - bly_ spend e - ter -
_ want you _ tryin' to get _ with me _ and I end up un -

Em7

- ni - ty. __ See,
- hap - py. __ I

F#m7

But if you_
So be - fore_

that's what you told _ me, that's what you said. _
don't need the hurt _ and I don't need the pain. _

Bm

_ want me _ you have _ to _ be _ ful - fill - ing all _
_ I do _ give my - self _ to _ you, _ I'll have to know_

1
Em7   F#m7
— my — dreams.—   If you real - ly want me, babe.   If —

2
Em7   F#m7
— the   truth —   if I spend my life   with   you. If —

Bm
— You   Had   My   Love   and   I   gave —

— you   all   my   trust   would   you   com -

Em7
fort ____ me?
(What would you   do, ___   babe?

F#m7   Bm
Tell me right now.) And if___ some-how you knew that your love_

— would   be   un - true   would   you   lie_

LOVE ME TENDER

Words and Music by
ELVIS PRESLEY and VERA MATSON

IN MY LIFE

Words and Music by
JOHN LENNON and PAUL McCARTNEY

Moderately

(Instrumental)

There are plac - es I'll re -
But of all these friends and

mem - ber all my life, _____ though
lov - ers there is no _____ one com -

some have changed.. Some for - ev - er, not for
pares with you. ___ And these mem - 'ries lose their

bet - ter; Some have gone _____ and
mean - ing when I think of _ love as

some re - main.. All these plac - es _ had _ their
some - thing new. _ Tho' I know I'll _ nev - er lose af -

mo - ments with lov - ers and friends _ I
fec - tion for peo - ple and things _ that

still can re-call. __ Some are dead _ and _ some _ are _
went _ be-fore, _ I know I'll of-ten stop and think a-

liv-ing, __ In My _____ Life I've
bout them, _ In My _____ Life I

loved them all. __ (Instrumental)
love you more. _

1.
2. D.S. al Coda
Tho' I

CODA
(Instrumental)
In

My _____ Life I love you

more.
(Instrumental)

ISN'T IT ROMANTIC?

from the Paramount Picture LOVE ME TONIGHT

Words by LORENZ HART
Music by RICHARD RODGERS

IT'S YOUR LOVE

Words and Music by
STEPHONY E. SMITH

Oh, it's a beau - ti - ful __ thing. __

__ Don't think I can keep it all __ in. __

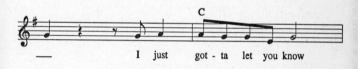

__ I just got - ta let you know

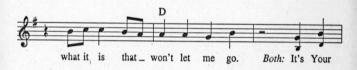

what it is that __ won't let me go. *Both:* It's Your

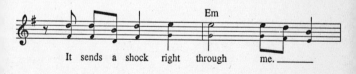

Love. __ It just does some-thin' to me.

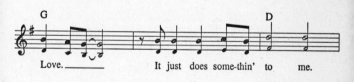

It sends a shock right through me. __

I can't __ get e - nough. __

And if you won - der___ a-bout the spell I'm

un - der, ___ *Male:* oh, ___ *Both:* It's

Your ___ Love. ___

Male: Bet-ter than I was, more than I am, ___

and all of this hap-pened by

tak-in' your hand. ___ And who I am now ___

is who I want-ed to be. *Both:* And

140

THE KEEPER OF THE STARS

Words and Music by KAREN STALEY,
DANNY MAYO and DICKEY LEE

Moderately Slow

It was _ no ac-ci-dent, _ me find-ing you.
Soft moon-light on your face, _ oh, how _ you shine.

Some-one had a hand in it _ long be-fore we ev-er knew.
It takes _ my _ breath a-way _ just to look _ in-to your eyes.

Now I _ just can't _ be-lieve _ you're in _ my life.
I know _ I don't _ de-serve _ a treas-ure _ like you.

Heav-en's smil-in' down on me _ as I look at you _ to-night.
There real-ly _ are no words _ to show my grat-i-tude.

So, I tip my hat
So, I tip my hat

LOVE OF A LIFETIME

Words and Music by BILL LEVERTY
and CARL SNARE

Slow Rock Ballad

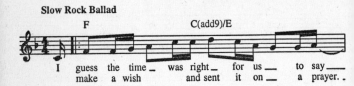

I guess the time was right for us to say
make a wish and sent it on a prayer.

we'd take our time and live our lives to-geth-
We know our dreams can all come true with

-er day by day. We'll
love that we can share. With

you I nev- er won- der,

"Will you be there for me?" With

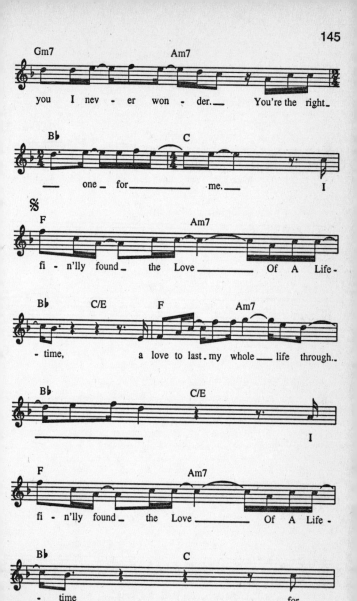

Gm7   Am7

know that we___ will___ be___ to - geth - er be -

Bb   C   D.S. al Coda

cause our love___ is _____ strong.___   I

CODA
F   C/E   Dm   C   Bb   F/A

- time.___

Gm7   C

Oo,_____   I

G   Bm7

fi - n'lly found___ the Love _____ Of A Life -

C   D/F#

- time, _____   a

G   Bm7

love to last___ my whole _____ life___ through..

148

fi - n'lly found the Love _____ Of A Life -

- time ___ for - ev - er in my heart. ___ I

fi - n'lly found the Love _____ Of A Life -

- time, _____ (Fi - n'lly found the Love _____ Of A Life -

Love _____ Of A Life -

- time.)

LOVE TAKES TIME

Words and Music by MARIAH CAREY
and BEN MARGULIES

I had it all _____ but I
Los - ing my mind _____ from this

let it _____ slip _____ a - way. _____
hol - low _____ in _____ my heart. _____

Could-n't see I treat - ed you wrong.
Sud-den-ly I'm so _____ in - complete, _____ yeah.

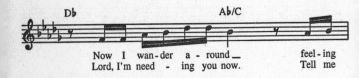

Now I wan-der a - round _____ feel-ing
Lord, I'm need - ing you now. Tell me

down _____ and cold _____
how _____ to stop the _____ rain.

MY FUNNY VALENTINE

from BABES IN ARMS

Words by LORENZ HART
Music by RICHARD RODGERS

My Fun-ny Val-en-tine, sweet com-ic

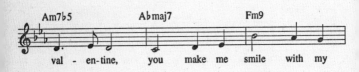

val-en-tine, you make me smile with my

heart. _____ Your looks are laugh-a-ble,

un-pho-to-graph-a-ble, yet, you're my

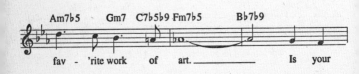

fav-'rite work of art. _____ Is your

MY HEART WILL GO ON

(Love Theme from 'Titanic')
from the Paramount and Twentieth Century Fox
Motion Picture TITANIC

Music by JAMES HORNER
Lyric by WILL JENNINGS

C#m   B(add9)

lieve   that   the   heart does   go

A   B   C#m

on.   Once

B   A   B

more   you   o - pen the door and you're

C#m   G#m   A

here   in my heart, and My Heart Will   Go

To Coda ⊕

Bsus   B   C#m7   Bsus

On   and   on.

A   Bsus   B E

Love   can touch us

B   Asus2   E/B   B

one time   and last for   a   life - time,

E   B   A

and nev-er let go till   we're gone.

E   B

Love   was when I   loved you;   one

Asus2   E/B G#7/B#   C#m

true time   I hold   to.   In my life we'll

G#m   A   D.S. al Coda

al - ways   go   on.

CODA

C#m7   Bsus

on. _____

A   Bsus   B

(Instrumental)

C#m7   Bsus

A   C#m/G# G#7/F#   Fm

You're

Eb   Db

here,   there's   noth - ing   I   fear

(You Make Me Feel Like)
A NATURAL WOMAN

Words and Music by GERRY GOFFIN,
CAROLE KING and JERRY WEXLER

162

SOMEONE LIKE YOU

from JEKYLL & HYDE

Words by LESLIE BRICUSSE
Music by FRANK WILDHORN

Slowly

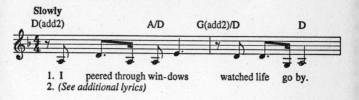

1. I peered through win-dows watched life go by.
2. *(See additional lyrics)*

Dreamed of to-mor-row, but stayed in-side.

The past was hold-ing me, keep-ing life at bay.

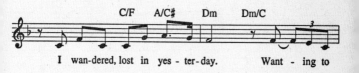

I wan-dered, lost in yes - ter-day. Want - ing to

fly, but scared to try. Then

164

CHORUS

ev - er   be the same.   My heart's tak - en   wing,___   and I

feel   so   a - live, _____   'cause

Slowly, freely

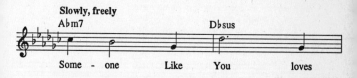

Some - one   Like   You   loves

me, _____   loves ___ me.

Additional Lyrics

2. It's like you took my dreams, made each one real,
   You reached inside of me and made me feel.
   And now I see a world I've never seen before.
   Your love has opened every door;
   You've set me free, now I can soar.

Chorus: For someone like you found someone like me.
   You touched my heart, nothing is the same.
   There's a new way to live, a new way to love,
   'Cause Someone Like You found me.

NOBODY LOVES ME LIKE YOU DO

Words by PAMELA PHILLIPS
Music by JAMES P. DUNNE

Do.

Do.

What if I nev-er met you? Where would I be right now?

Fun-ny how life just falls in place some-how. You

touched my heart in plac-es that I nev-er e-ven knew..

No - bod - y Loves Me Like You Do.

No-bod-y loves me, no-bod-y loves me,

No - bod - y Loves Me Like You Do.

No-bod-y Loves Me Like You Do.

PRECIOUS AND FEW

Words and Music by
WALTER D. NIMS

Moderately

Pre - cious And Few____ are the mo - ing
Ba - by it's you____ on my mind ___

- ments we two can share;
___ your love is so rare;

qui - et and blue __ like the sky ___ I've hung o - ver you.
be - ing with you__ is a feel - ing I just can't com - pare..

And if I
And if I

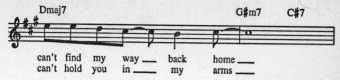

can't find my way ___ back home ___
can't hold you in ___ my arms ___

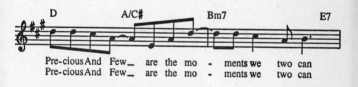

it just would-n't be fair, ___ 'cause
it just would-n't be fair, ___ 'cause

Pre-cious And Few ___ are the mo - ments we two can
Pre-cious And Few ___ are the mo - ments we two can

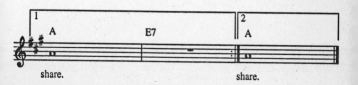

share.   share.

REMEMBER ME THIS WAY

from the Universal Motion Picture CASPER

Music by DAVID FOSTER
Lyrics by LINDA THOMPSON

Moderately slow

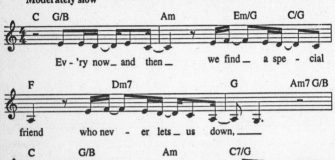

Ev - 'ry now and then we find a spe - cial

friend who nev - er lets us down, who

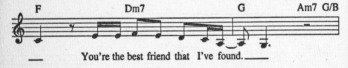

who un-der-stands it all, reach-es out each time you fall.

You're the best friend that I've found.

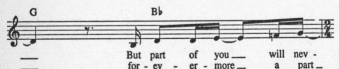

I know you can't stay.
And I know that you'll be there,

But part of you will nev -
for - ev - er - more a part

172

RIBBON IN THE SKY

Words and Music by
STEVIE WONDER

Slowly, with expression

Eb m7   Fm7   Bb 7sus

Oh, so long ____ for this night I prayed ____ that a
lowed, ____ may I touch your hand, ____ and if

Eb m7   Fm7   Bb 7sus

star ____ would guide you my way ____ to share
pleased ____ may I once a - gain, so that

Eb m7   Fm7   Bb 7sus

with ____ me this spe - cial day ____ where a
you ____ too will un - der - stand ____ there's a

1   Ebm11 Ebm/F Ebm/Gb Eb/G Ab7sus   Cbmaj7   Ab7sus

rib - bon's in the sky for our love. ____ If al -

2   Ebm11 Ebm/F Ebm/Gb Eb/G Ab7sus   Db

rib - bon in the sky for our love. ____ Doo
(Vocal ad lib.)

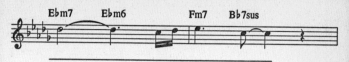

doo doo _____

_____ doo doo _____

_____ doo _____ doo. _____

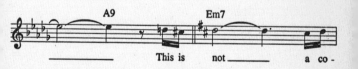

_____ This is not _____ a co-

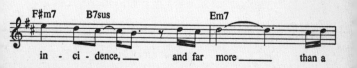

in - ci - dence, _____ and far more _____ than a

luck - y chance, ___ but what is _____ that was

al - ways meant ___ is our rib - bon in the sky for our love,.

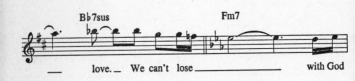

___ love. ___ We can't lose _____ with God

on our side. ___ We'll find strength ___ in each

tear we cry. ___ From now on _____ it will be

you and I ___ and our rib - bon in the sky,

rib-bon in the sky, a rib - bon in the sky for our love..

— Ooh, ___ ooh ooh. ___
(Vocal ad lib.)

Doo doo _____

_____ ooh ____

_____ There's a

rib - bon in the sky for our love._____

SAVE THE BEST FOR LAST

Words and Music by PHIL GALDSTON,
JON LIND and WENDY WALDMAN

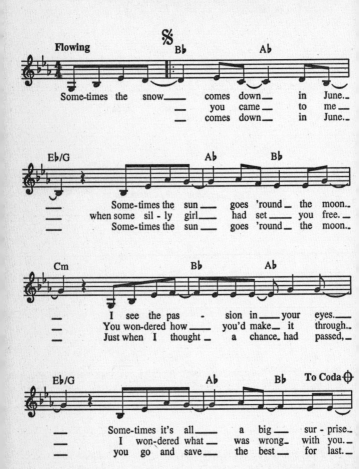

Some-times the snow____ comes down____ in June..
____ you came____ to me____
____ comes down____ in June..

____ Some-times the sun____ goes 'round____ the moon..
____ when some sil - ly girl____ had set____ you free..
____ Some-times the sun____ goes 'round____ the moon..

____ I see the pas - sion in____ your eyes.
____ You won-dered how____ you'd make____ it through.
____ Just when I thought____ a chance, had passed,

____ Some-times it's all____ a big____ sur - prise.
____ I won-dered what____ was wrong____ with you..
____ you go and save____ the best____ for last..

179

180

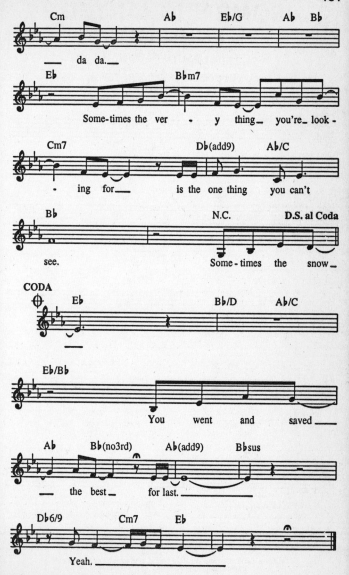

SOME ENCHANTED EVENING

from SOUTH PACIFIC

Lyrics by OSCAR HAMMERSTEIN II
Music by RICHARD RODGERS

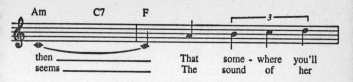

then _____ That some - where you'll
seems _____ The sound of her

see her a - gain and a
laugh - ter will sing in your

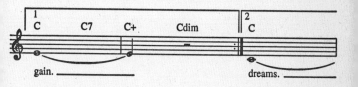

1.
gain. _____

2.
dreams. _____

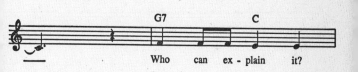

_____ Who can ex - plain it?

Who can tell you why? Fools give you rea - sons,

Wise men nev-er try. ____

Some En-chant-ed Eve - ning ____

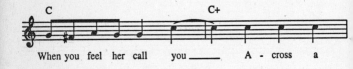

When you find your true love, ____

When you feel her call you ____ A - cross a

crowd - ed room, Then fly to her

185

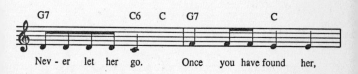

SOMETHING

Words and Music by
GEORGE HARRISON

Slowly

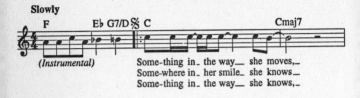

(Instrumental)

Some-thing in_ the way_ she moves,_
Some-where in_ her smile_ she knows_
Some-thing in_ the way_ she knows,_

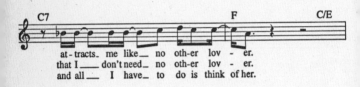

at - tracts_ me like_ no oth-er lov - er.
that I ___ don't need_ no oth-er lov - er.
and all ___ I have_ to do is think of her.

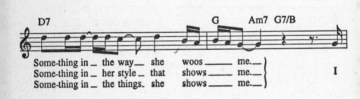

Some-thing in_ the way_ she woos ___ me._
Some-thing in_ her style_ that shows ___ me._
Some-thing in_ the things_ she shows ___ me._

I

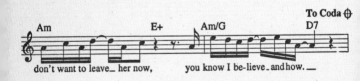

To Coda

don't want to leave_ her now, you know I be-lieve_ and how. __

(Instrumental) ... *(Instrumental)*

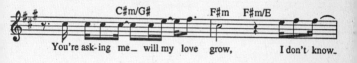

You're ask-ing me __ will my love grow, I don't know __

__ I __ don't know. You stick a-round_ now, it may

show, I don't know __ I __ don't know.

D.S. al Coda

CODA

(Instrumental)

SOMETIMES WHEN WE TOUCH

Words by DAN HILL
Music by BARRY MANN

Slowly, in 2

You ask me if ___ I love ___
mance and all ___ its strat-
times I un - der-stand

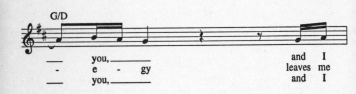

___ you, ___ and I
- e - gy leaves me
___ you, ___ and I

choke on my ___ re - ply. ___
bat - tling with ___ my pride. ___
know how hard ___ you've tried.

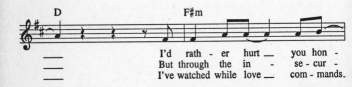

___ I'd rath - er hurt ___ you hon -
___ But through the in - se - cur -
___ I've watched while love ___ com - mands.

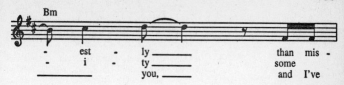

- est - ly _____ than mis-
- i - ty _____ some
you, _____ and I've

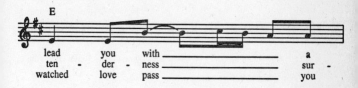

lead you with _____ a
ten - der - ness _____ sur-
watched love pass _____ you

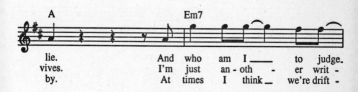

lie. And who am I _____ to judge.
vives. I'm just an - oth - er writ-
by. At times I think _____ we're drift-

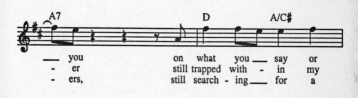

_____ you on what you _____ say or
- er still trapped with - in my
- ers, still search - ing _____ for a

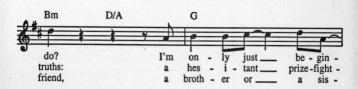

do? I'm on - ly just _____ be - gin-
truths: a hes - i - tant _____ prize-fight-
friend, a broth - er or _____ a sis-

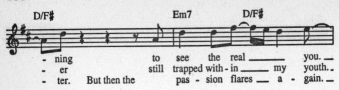

- ning   to   see   the   real _____ you. __
- er   still   trapped with-in _____ my   youth..
- ter.   But then the   pas - sion flares ___ a - gain. __

And Some-times When We Touch,.

the   hon - es - ty's ___ too ___ much,.

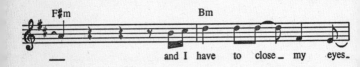

and I   have   to   close ___ my   eyes.

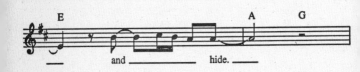

and _____ hide. ___

I   wan - na   hold   you   till ___ I   die, _

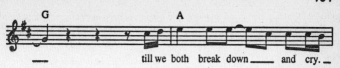

till we both break down ___ and cry. ___

I wan-na hold you till the fear ___

in me ___ sub -

sides. *(Instrumental)*

Ro -

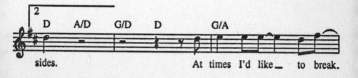

sides. At times I'd like ___ to break.

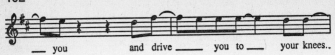

_ you and drive _ you to _ your knees..

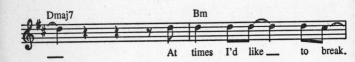

Dmaj7   Bm

_ At times I'd like _ to break.

F#m   G

_ through _ and hold _ you end - less-ly. _

G/A   D.S. al Coda

At

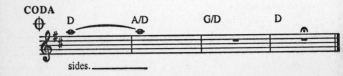

CODA
D   A/D   G/D   D

sides. _____

THE SWEETEST DAYS

Words and Music by JON LIND,
PHIL GALDSTON and WENDY WALDMAN

Slow Ballad

You and I ____ in this mo - ment, ____
There are times ____ that scare ____ me. ____ We'll

hold - ing the night ____ so ____ close,
rat - tle the house ____ like the wind,

hang - ing on, ____ still un - bro - ken ____ while
both of us ____ so un - bend - ing. ____ We

out - side the thun - der ____ rolls. ____
bat - tle the fear ____ with - in. ____

Lis - ten now, you can hear ____ my heart - beat
All the while life is rush - ing by ____ us.

warm a - gainst life's bit - ter cold. ____ } These are ____ the days, ____
Hold it now and don't let go. ____

194

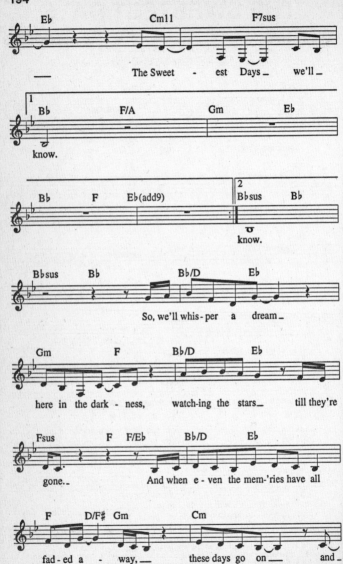

The Sweet - est Days — we'll —

[1] know.

know.

So, we'll whis - per a dream —

here in the dark - ness, watch-ing the stars — till they're

gone. — And when e - ven the mem-'ries have all

fad - ed a - way, — these days go on — and —

THREE TIMES A LADY

Words and Music by
LIONEL RICHIE

Slowly

Ab / Ab/Gb / Fm

Thanks for the times that you've giv - en me __

C7#5/E / Ab / Ab/Gb

The mem-'ries __ are all __ in my mind __

Fm / C7#5/E / Ab

And now that we've

Ab/Gb / Fm / C7#5/E

come to the end of our rain - bow

Ab / Ab/Gb / Fm

there's some-thing I must __ say out __ loud: _____

C7#5/E / Ab

You're once,

A TIME FOR US
(Love Theme)
from the Paramount Picture ROMEO AND JULIET

Words by LARRY KUSIK and EDDIE SNYDER
Music by NINO ROTA

Slowly and expressively

A Time For Us some-day there'll be when chains are torn by cour-age born of a love that's free. A time when dreams so long de-nied _____ can flour - ish _____ as we un-veil the love we now must

hide. _____ A Time _____ For

Us _____ at last _____ to

see _____ a life _____ worth -

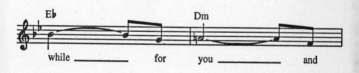

while _____ for you _____ and

me. And with our love through tears and

thorns we will en - dure as we pass

202

sure - ly through ev - 'ry storm. A Time For

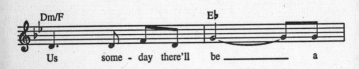

Us some - day there'll be _____ a

new world, _____ a

world of shin - ing hope for you and

me. A Time For me.

TO LOVE YOU MORE

Words and Music by DAVID FOSTER and JUNIOR MILES

Slowly, half-time feel

Take me ___ back in - to the arms I love. ___ Need me like you did be - fore. ___ Touch me once a - gain ___ and re - mem - ber when ___ there was no one that you want - ed more.

Don't   go,   you __ know   you'll
See   me   as __ if   you

break   my   heart.
nev - er know. _____

She   won't   love   you __ like   I
Hold   me   so   you __ can't   let

will. _____   I'm   the   one   who'll stay __
go. _____   Just be - lieve in   me. __

____   when   she   walks a - way, __
____   I   will make   you   see __

____   and   you   know __ I'll be stand -
____   all   the   things __ that your heart __

- ing   here   still. _____ }
  needs to   know. _____ }

I'll be   wait - ing for you __

here in - side _ my heart._

I'm the one _ who wants _ To Love_

You _ More. _

(1.,2.) { You will }
(D.S.) { Can't you } see I can give _

_ you _ ev - 'ry - thing _ you need._

Let me be _ the one To Love_

You _ More. _

And some way, _

all the love ___ that we had can be saved. ___

What-ev-er it takes, ___

we'll find ___ a way. ___

(Instrumental)

Be - lieve in me.

I will make you see all the things ___

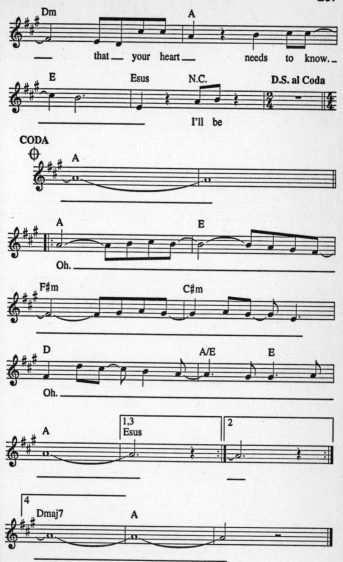

TRUE LOVE

from HIGH SOCIETY

Words and Music by
COLE PORTER

Slowly   G   C

I   give   to   you   and   you

C#dim7   G   D7

give   to   me   True

C   G

Love,   True   Love.   So,

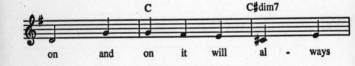

C   C#dim7

on   and   on   it   will   al - ways

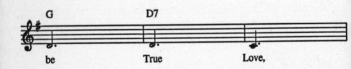

G   D7

be   True   Love,

True Love. For you and

I have a guard - ian an - gel on

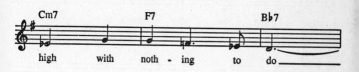

high with noth - ing to do ____

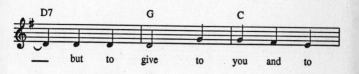

____ but to give to you and to

give to me love for -

ev - er true. ____

UNCHAINED MELODY
from the Motion Picture UNCHAINED

Lyric by HY ZARET
Music by ALEX NORTH

212

UP WHERE WE BELONG

**from the Paramount Picture
AN OFFICER AND A GENTLEMAN**

Words by WILL JENNINGS
Music by BUFFY SAINTE-MARIE and JACK NITZSCHE

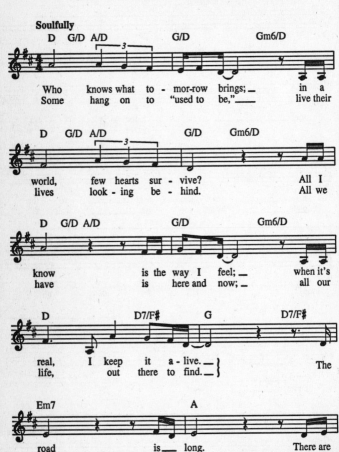

VALENTINE

Words and Music by JACK KUGELL
and JIM BRICKMAN

Smoothly

If there were no words,___ no way to speak,___
All of my life, I have been wait -

— ing for ___ I ___ would still ___ hear ___ you.
all ___ you give ___ to ___ me.

If there were no tears,___ no way to feel
You've o - pened my eyes ___ and shown me how___

— in - side, ___ I'd still ___ feel for ___ you. And
to love ___ un - self - ish - ly. ___ I've

(1.,D.S.) e - ven if the sun ___ re - fused ___ to shine,___
(2.) dreamed of this a thou - sand times ___ be - fore,___

217

la,   la,   la,___   la,   la.___

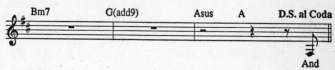

And

___   my Val - en - tine.___

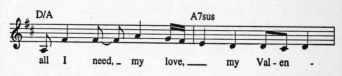

___   Oh,___   oh.___   You're

all I   need,_ my love,___   my Val - en -

tine.   Oh,___

oh.___

WHEN I FALL IN LOVE

Words by EDWARD HEYMAN
Music by VICTOR YOUNG

WHEN YOU SAY NOTHING AT ALL

Words and Music by DON SCHLITZ
and PAUL OVERSTREET

It's a-maz - ing how you
All day long I can hear

can speak right to my heart.
peo-ple talk - ing out loud,

With-out say - ing a word
but when you hold me near

you can light up the dark.
you drown out the crowd.

Try as I may I could nev-
Old Mis-ter Web-ster could nev-

When You Say Noth-ing At All. ____

(Instrumental)

D.S. al Coda

The

CODA

When You Say Noth - ing At All. __

(Instrumental)

A WHOLE NEW WORLD

from Walt Disney's ALADDIN

Music by ALAN MENKEN
Words by TIM RICE

WILL YOU LOVE ME TOMORROW
(Will You Still Love Me Tomorrow)

Words and Music by GERRY GOFFIN
and CAROLE KING

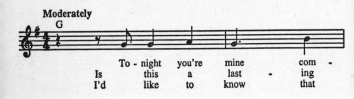

To - night you're mine com -
Is this a last - ing
I'd like to know that

plete - ly,
treas - ure,
your _____ love

you give your love so
or just a mo - ment's
is love I can be

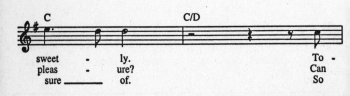

sweet - ly. To -
pleas - ure? Can
sure _____ of. So

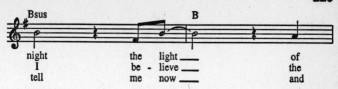

night   the   light _____   of
I   be - lieve _____   the
tell   me   now _____   and

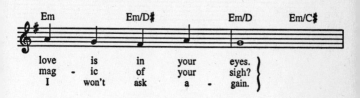

love   is   in   your   eyes.
mag - ic   of   your   sigh?
I   won't ask   a - gain.

Will   You   Still   Love   Me   To -

mor - row?

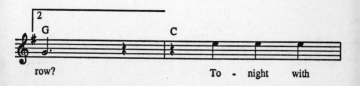

row?   To - night with

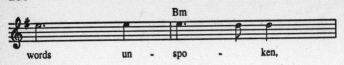

words   un - spo - ken,

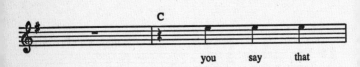

you   say   that

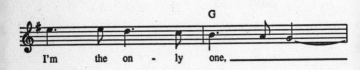

I'm   the   on - ly   one, _____

_   but   will   my

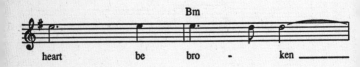

heart   be   bro - ken _____

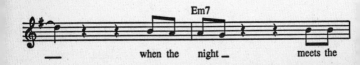

_   when the   night _   meets the

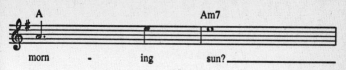

morn - ing   sun?_____

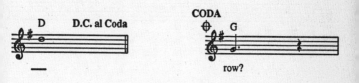

D   D.C. al Coda   CODA   G

—   row?

C   C/D

Will   You   Still   Love   Me   To -

N.C.   Em   Em/D#

mor   -   row? (Instrumental)

Em/D   Em/C#   C

D   G

YOU MEAN THE WORLD TO ME

Words and Music by BABYFACE, L.A. REID and DARYL SIMMONS

Moderately

If you could give me one good rea - son
gon - na take some work - in' but

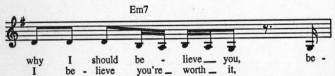

why I should be - lieve___ you, be -
I be - lieve you're___ worth___ it,

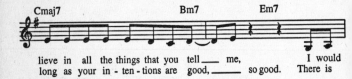

lieve in all the things that you tell ___ me, I would
long as your in - ten - tions are good, _____ so good. There is

sure like to be - lieve___ you. My heart wants to re - ceive you. Just
just one way to show___ it and, boy, I hope you know it, that

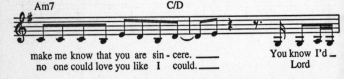

make me know that you are sin - cere. ___ You know I'd
no one could love you like I could. ___ Lord

Am7

— me how you feel, ba - by, I'm for real, oh,

baby, ba - by, ba - by, ba - by, ba - by.___

Ebmaj7

C/D

— 'Cause You Mean The World___

G   G/F

— To Me, you are my ev - 'ry-thing, I swear the on -

C/E   Ebmaj7   Eb6

- ly thing that mat-ters, mat-ters to me. Oh,

G   C#m7b5

baby, ba - by, ba - by, ba - by, baby, ___ 'cause you mean so

Am7   C/D   Repeat and Fade

much   to___ me.   You Mean The World___

YOU NEEDED ME

Words and Music by
RANDY GOODRUM

Slowly

I cried a tear, you wiped it dry. I was con-
hand when it was cold. When I was

fused, you cleared my mind. I sold my soul, you bought it
lost, you took me home. You gave me hope, when I was

back for me ___ and held me up and gave me
at the end, ___ and turned my lies back in-to

dig-ni-ty. ___ Some-how You Need-ed Me.
truth a-gain. ___ You e-ven called me friend. } You gave me

strength to stand a-lone a-gain ___ to face the world out on my

own a-gain. ___ You put me high up-on a ped-es-tal, ___ so

YOU WERE MEANT FOR ME

Words and Music by JEWEL KILCHER
and STEVE POLTZ

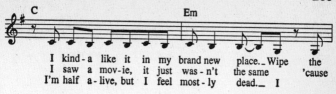

C   Em

I kind-a like it in my brand new   place. Wipe the
I saw a mov-ie, it just was-n't   the same   'cause
I'm half a-live, but I feel most-ly   dead. I

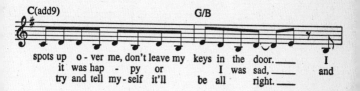

C(add9)   G/B

spots up o-ver me, don't leave my keys in the door.   I
it was hap - py or   I was sad,   and
try and tell my-self it'll   be all   right.

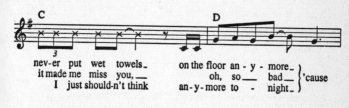

C   D

nev-er put wet towels   on the floor an - y - more
it made me miss you,   oh, so   bad   } 'cause
I just should-n't think   an-y-more to - night

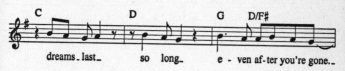

C   D   G   D/F#

dreams last   so long   e - ven af-ter you're gone.

Em7 Em7/D   C   D

   I know   that you love me, and

G   D/F#   Em   Em/D

soon   you   will see   You Were Meant

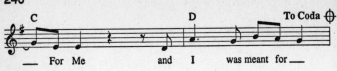

_ For Me and I was meant for _

you. I

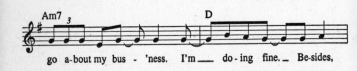

go a-bout my bus - 'ness. I'm _ do-ing fine. _ Be-sides,

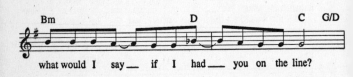

what would I say _ if I had _ you on the line?

Same old sto - ry, not much to say. _

Freely

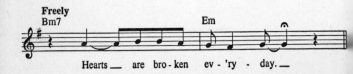

Hearts _ are bro-ken ev - 'ry - day. _

Tempo primo

(Instrumental)

you.

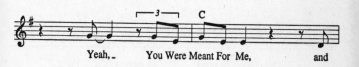

Yeah,___ You Were Meant For Me, and

I was meant for you.___

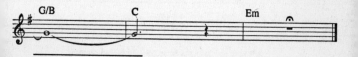

YOU'LL BE IN MY HEART

(Pop Version)
from Walt Disney Pictures' TARZAN™

Words and Music by
PHIL COLLINS

Come stop your cry-ing; it will be all right.

Just take my hand, hold it tight.

I will pro-tect you from all a-round you.

I will be here; don't you cry.

For one so small you seem so strong.
Why can't they un-der-stand the way we feel?

My arms will hold you, keep you
They just don't trust what they

safe and warm.
can't ex - plain.

244

Cm   Ab(add2)

be here in ___ my ___ heart   al -

Db   Bb7sus   Ab   Bb   D.S. al Coda

- ways.   *(Instrumental)*

CODA

Bb   Absus   Ab

Don't   lis-ten to them, ___   'cause
        des-ti-ny calls ___ you   you

Absus2   Ab   What do they know? ___
                   Got-ta be strong. ___

what do they ___ know? ___   We
must ___ be ___ strong. ___   It

Absus/F   Fm7

need each oth-er   to
may not be with you,   but you've

Absus/F   Fm7

have, to ___ hold. ___ }
got to hold ___ on. ___

They'll ___

Cm7

___ see ___ in time,   I ___

[1]   Db

___ know. ___   When

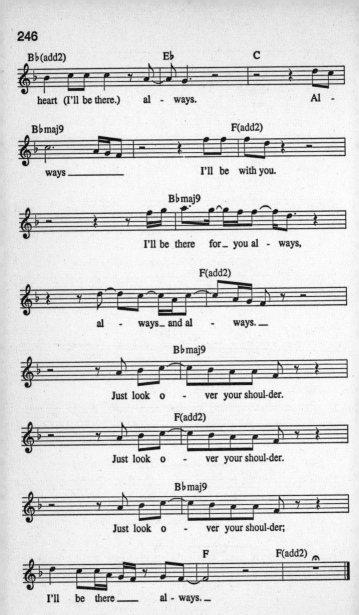

YOU'VE GOT A FRIEND

Words and Music by
CAROLE KING

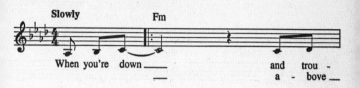

Slowly   Fm

When you're down ___   and trou -
___   a - bove

C7/G   Fm   C7

- bled,   and you need ___ some love and care;
___ you   grows ___ dark ___ and full of clouds;

Fm/Ab   C7/G   Fm   Bbm7

And   noth - in'
And   that ol'

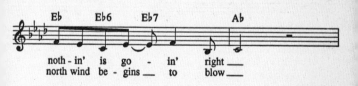

Eb   Eb6   Eb7   Ab

noth - in' is go - in' right ___
north wind be - gins ___ to blow ___

Bbm/Ab   Ab   Gm7

close   your   eyes ___ and
keep   your   head ___ to -

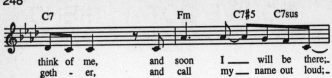

C7   Fm   C7#5 C7sus

think of me,   and soon   I __ will be there;_
geth - er,   and call   my __ name out loud;_

Fm/Ab C7sus Fm   Bbm7

To bright - en up __   e - me -
Soon you'll hear __   me -

Cm7   Db6/Eb Eb

- ven your dark - est night.__ }
- knock - in' at __ your door.__ }

Db6/Eb   𝄋 Ab

You just call __   out my __ name,_

Db

_   and you know__ wher - ev - er I am_

Ab

_   I'll come run - nin'_____

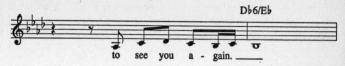

to see you a - gain. ____

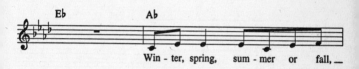

Win - ter, spring, sum - mer or fall, __

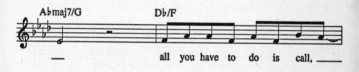

__ all you have to do is call, ____

and I'll be __

__ there. _____ You've Got A Friend.

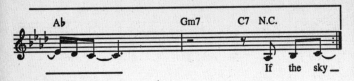

Ab   **Gm7**   **C7**   **N.C.**

If the sky __

2   **Db**   **Cm7**   **Bbm7** **Db6/Eb**

__ there, __ yes, I will. _____ Now

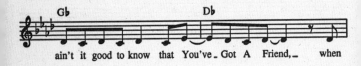

Gb   **Db**

ain't it good to know that You've _ Got A Friend, _ when

Ab   **Abmaj7**

peo - ple can be __ so cold. __ They'll hurt _

Db   **Gb7**

__ you, yes, and de - sert __ you, and

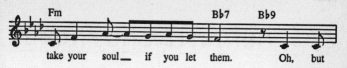

Fm   Bb7   Bb9

take your soul___ if you let them.   Oh, but

Bbm7/Eb   Eb   D.S. al Coda

don't you let___ them.   You just call___

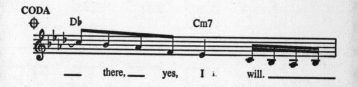

CODA

Db   Cm7

___ there,___ yes, I   will. _____

Bbm7 Db6/Eb   Ab   Db/Ab

___ You've Got A Friend. ___   You've Got A

Ab   Db/Ab   **Repeat and Fade**

Friend. ___   Ain't it good___ to know You've Got A

GUITAR CHORD FRAMES

	C	Cm	C+	C6	Cm6
C					

	C#	C#m	C#+	C#6	C#m6
C#/D♭					

	D	Dm	D+	D6	Dm6
D					

	E♭	E♭m	E♭+	E♭6	E♭m6
E♭/D#					

	E	Em	E+	E6	Em6
E					

	F	Fm	F+	F6	Fm6
F					

This guitar chord reference includes 120 commonly used chords. For a more complete guide to guitar chords, see "THE PAPERBACK CHORD BOOK" (HL00702009).

	C7	Cmaj7	Cm7	C7sus	Cdim7
C					

	C#7	C#maj7	C#m7	C#7sus	C#dim7
C#/Db					

	D7	Dmaj7	Dm7	D7sus	Ddim7
D					

	Eb7	Ebmaj7	Ebm7	Eb7sus	Ebdim7
Eb/D#					

	E7	Emaj7	Em7	E7sus	Edim7
E					

	F7	Fmaj7	Fm7	F7sus	Fdim7
F					

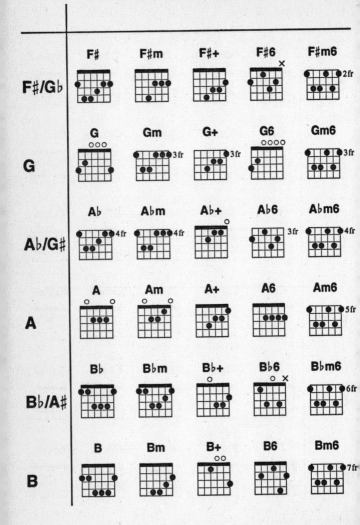

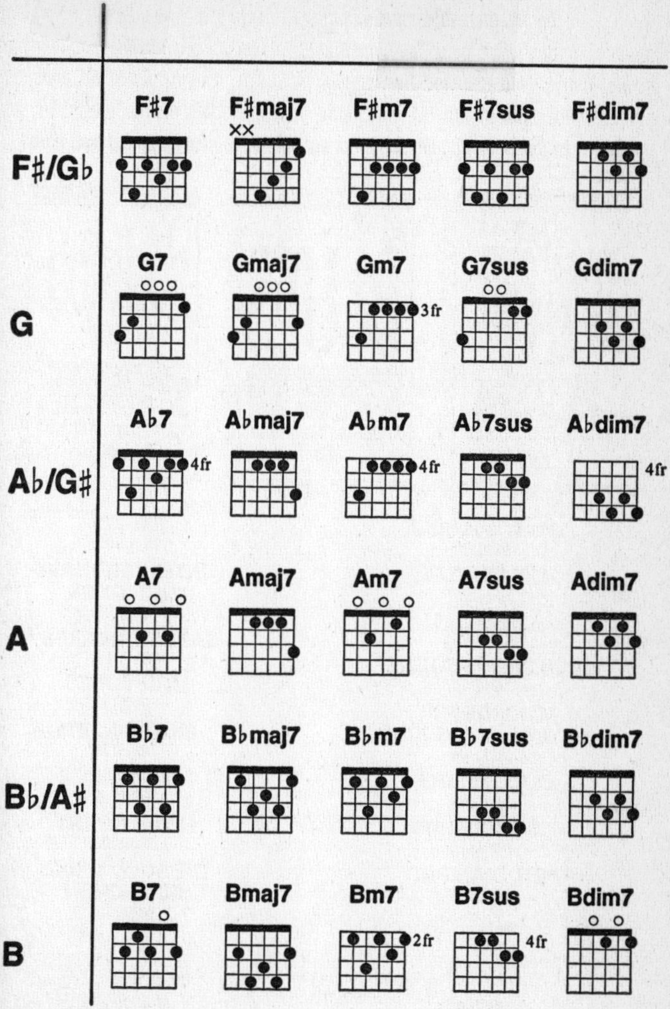
F♯/G♭
F♯7
F♯maj7
F♯m7
F♯7sus
F♯dim7
G
G7
Gmaj7
Gm7
3fr
G7sus
Gdim7
A♭/G♯
A♭7
4fr
A♭maj7
A♭m7
4fr
A♭7sus
A♭dim7
4fr
A
A7
Amaj7
Am7
A7sus
Adim7
B♭/A♯
B♭7
B♭maj7
B♭m7
B♭7sus
B♭dim7
B
B7
Bmaj7
Bm7
2fr
B7sus
4fr
Bdim7

THE PAPERBACK SONGS SERIES

These perfectly portable paperbacks include the melodies, lyrics, and chords symbols for your favorite songs, all in a convenient, pocket-sized book. Using concise, one-line music notation, anyone from hobbyists to professionals can strum on the guitar, play melodies on the piano, or sing the lyrics to great songs. Books also include a helpful guitar chord chart.

'80s & '90s ROCK 00240126	**HYMNS** 00240103
THE BEATLES 00702008	**INTERNATIONAL FOLKSONGS** 00240104
THE BLUES 00702014	**JAZZ STANDARDS** 00240114
CHILDREN'S SONGS 00240149	**LOVE SONGS** 00240150
CHORDS FOR KEYBOARD & GUITAR 00702009	**MOTOWN HITS** 00240125
CLASSIC ROCK 00310058	**MOVIE MUSIC** 00240113
COUNTRY HITS 00702013	**ELVIS PRESLEY** 00240102
NEIL DIAMOND 00702012	**THE ROCK & ROLL COLLECTION** 00702020

FOR MORE INFORMATION, SEE YOUR LOCAL MUSIC DEALER,
OR WRITE TO:

HAL•LEONARD®
C O R P O R A T I O N
7777 W. BLUEMOUND RD. P.O. BOX 13819 MILWAUKEE, WI 53213

Prices, availability and contents subject to change without notice.
Some products may not be available outside the U.S.A.